Tattvas

Anne Bateman

Published by Cinnamon Press.
www.cinnamonpress.com

ISBN 978-1-78864-150-0

British Library Cataloguing in Publication Data. A CIP record for this book can be obtained from the British Library.

Designed and typeset in Bodoni by Cinnamon Press. Cover design by Adam Craig.

Cinnamon Press is represented by Inpress Ltd.

Author Biography

Anne Bateman has spent her life teaching and travelling in North Africa, Nepal, Spain and France, where she now lives, teaching yoga and meditation.

She studied English literature at Ulster University during the civil war. Since then, she has been preoccupied with our differing perspectives and the stories we tell ourselves.

She is the author of *My Body Remembers* and is a Kith mentee.

Contents

For Georgina, a lifetime of friendship, feedback and encouragement,
Duncan, Martha and Jan, for their guidance to the source,
for Mum and my early immersion in her love of poetry,
and for Steve, Zoe, Louis and Dan and all the love we feel for each other.

Tattvas

Earth

From dust to dirt

however much we toil
there is no end
only this ever present
raising dust

sweeping reeds across the floor,
bare feet rootling in smooth earth
damp cloths reveal matter made new
brass buffed to an untarnished shine

—hedging time

while outside in all
that tended symmetry
a rush of dandelions
their double-headed suns
in a mandala of bitter leaves,

roots tapping deep
flowers chasing light in a karaoke blaze,
rejected for the posies
turn to fragile geometry
and empty on a breath

Tasting the earth

we fell into step
path worn into rock,
cloud spilling over the col,

into the forest, moss
on every surface north,
coughing up blood,

and with more days
of hard walking ahead
before she reached the hospital,

through apple orchards,
tasting mustard oil,
woodsmoke in the air,

turning the screw,
sharing pressed juice
too fast to savour,

and from between her breasts,
she brought out boiled potatoes,
tasting of earth

The Field

the view is boundless green
—   garden to field to wall of oak

where keening red kites nest
and other animal calls sound

—   deer and boar, hunted in autumn,
race and bleed on barbed wire,

so when the farmer steps back,
leaving the earth to reknit,

it breathes each blade's push to
catch light, a refracting

waist-high churning, a summer pelt
of silk sliding on wind.

No more rivers of black slugs
fleeing a chemical dissolution,

but a border of buttercups,
flanking barbed wire,

and as the dawn dew draws down
grass heads, heavy with drenching

each stem threads an arc of droplets,
multiple moons—crescents of reflected sky

Rock

there's a scramble, grazing
grit-pitted pumice too hot to touch

and fear of one misstep
to unbalance, one misplaced grip tipping

stone and flesh falling
pinned by weight but still alive

to the sea thrashing through fallen boulders
sliding through shallows, shells sharp as razors

and just in time, a hand searching
to steady stops as

a tiny crab scuttles side on
into shelter

I am earth

nobody told me about this late flowering
the tender explosion felt in heart and head

mirrors, or being held in the gaze of others
can no longer hurt and there are remedies

shimmering in the body, if we would only
believe and move and breathe into them

I am earth, fed, watered and turned
become a garden, bigger than myself

Water

Rockpool

in the narrow sea
you can hardly call them waves,
shallow panting licks,

even so there are
perfect zen gardens scoured smooth
where each wave has churned

rocks round, nestled in
brimming bowls of salt water
open to the sky.

Even...

the wasps are thirsty
in the crawlspace of the tap
waiting for water

waking in the night
the air is so still, it seems
everything is dead

Lake

waterlilies bounce
in your flotsam-strewn wake.

the lake is alive, breathing
bubbles, breaking the surface,

and my arms, foreshortened,
comb through liquid,

sunset
pink through the poplars.

There's the splash
of a fish falling

as cold feet dredge
the lake's underbelly

River

dippers bounce and swing on the wind,
strafing the glittering
as the river breaks, slipping smooth
over rocks,

facing down the current, a trout
hangs in the green ice-melt,
and dragonflies sweep shallows
where back-eddies stink.

                  As curfew lifts,
there is the distant drone of traffic,
a cast line splashes as the lure hits,
and we shade our eyes

against the black burn of the sun,
seeing a heron flap out of the weeds,
barely lifting, flying
              to the opposite bank of darkness

Fire

Sennar

we are listening to each other

I know he is squatting,
on the other side of the door,
arm sweeping in semi circles
driving the dust of the night
across the cold-tiled floor

there is also probably
the call to prayer buzzing
through my bones

and outside, in the early morning,
schoolgirls link arms,
lean against each other,
languid in careless connection,
hennaed fingers punctuating each exchange.

they laugh, mimicking my fast strut

I haven't yet learned to move slowly
through this warm bath of air

Sunrise

tottering on high
heels, leggy up-all-night girls,
and the elderly

wrapped in towels,
the wind cold off the sea,
sky growing

lighter, a promise
blushing where sea meets
sky and over the grey land

a salt breeze lifts
and the tip of the sun's
tongue tastes the light

Noon

when shadows eat themselves
as air pulses with heavy heat
singing treble,

a rustle of scales
drawn across dry leaves whisper
its being at the edge of sight

where a flick of narrow tail
whipping behind rock
suggests a sinuous body

paused mid-dart,
stretched poised
sprung on reach

Air

Fana

at dusk as we turn to face any breeze,
needles pointing north
in this hot season,

chairs are dragged
to the place which teases
breeze from becalmed,

we are bellying sails, reeds
blown by the wind, music
heard in our skin,

felt
in the nape's downy hair
shiver of pleasure

Feather

this feather
separates us from flight so
land-lubbered, we crawl,

while this membrane, strong
enough to bear down on air
to lift, soar and dive

without ripping and
soft enough to waft, traces
shivers in its tip

Wind

even the poplars,
their leaves
incessant flapping dappling
from shadow to light

The Nightjar

slender wings carving
air on its electric
jagged flight, scooping

insects hovering
at dusk across
the eye of the lake

Opening

we arrive at our own
chosen end,
doors closing behind

and falling back into soft grass,
find all this sky
not seen since childhood,

where clouds seem caught
in a still shot of trailing,
bunching into mass

and a kite dips
as if to check out
the flailing,

while a blackbird runs up scales
of charge and flow, so near,
the sound pours

through flowering nerves
and I remember to open
my arms to all that blue

Akasha

Kina Aeko

between the head strap and the rock she rests on,
balances a basket of foraged firewood
leaning forward,
taking the strain in neck and legs,
she climbs home

I follow slowly, climbing all day, panting the thin air,
skin hot and cold from sun and wind,
breath settling to match each step

out of the sea of cloud we move
past ragged spines of fissured rock
thrusting into infinity, red magma,
a whiff of iron in old blood, exhaled from the earth's heart
sheer below us, scatter of fallen boulders,
pulled down by time and gravity

eyes down, negotiating uneven footfall
past the names of god, carved into rock,
in the presence of something
prayer wheels in the streams
prayer flags in the wind
up to the snowline
where silence screams
to the peace beyond, where nothing lives

a high cold valley, two weeks from the nearest road,
wood smoke from a house, mud floor tamped by bare feet,
hand-beaten brass, a sugary tea

a mother sits in the sun, baby in lap;
terraces hewn with stone-honed metal
sweep to the floor of the valley

she leans forward, face next to her baby,
pointing to the valley,
a house,
a tree,
a bird
I watch her show her child the world

Kina aeko? she asks me
Why have you come?

Love

and when my breasts
no longer quickened with milk
when any baby cried,

one after the other
they took their first steps away
trusting momentum,

fearless of gravity—
I would have done anything
to keep them happy.

Baby Krishna, baby Jesus,
such an intense lesson
we are all one,

coming through birthing to survive,
and when they asked me
What is stronger… a leaf or a lion?

rock or water? wind or fire?
my answers, hedged with examples
confused them

So what's the strongest thing in the world?
I knew this one; no hesitation, *Love*
but forgot, kept busy…
got things done

clambering along the roof
in a gusting crosswind
body tensed the better to take

the futility of certainties
hammering the fixings
against the wind lifting each corner

ripping the building roofless
feet braced against falling
braking, holding on

weaving through the oncoming crowd
I release my children
from an outdated pushchair

to run in open spaces
they climb the stairs again and again
mastering the skills to escape

Counting the inheritance

spoons—worn to a lopsided angle,
curling brownie snapshots
corners unsticking,

and my grandmother, for whom I am named,
carrying me
in my mother's unborn body

packed her bags and left—
her children watching from the dark
at the top of the stairs,

seeing their world
shut behind her, returning
half an hour later

saying
there is nowhere to go,
but kept going, quietly

feeding wet clothes into the mangle,
streaming hot suds into the copper, a child
straining to turn the handle,

and in the house, the wall
of cold, as heavy as piled blankets pressing
 on my child's body in the narrow bed

—evenings, we nestled
into each other, in the one room
with the one fire,

poker flaming blue
into a mound of moulded coke,
hissing, hearing

footsteps nearing home,
where shade and light flicker,
thrumming wings,

holding to stillness
at the mouth of the flower, beating
of mothers and their mothers' hearts

From the four corners drawn here

the distant spire rising from the plain calls
from the bypass, a chance entering into the cool shafts
of light, above, shadowy oak-bolstered vaults,
and underfoot, toad-cold marble,
while at eye level, range orchestras and choirs
in tiers, a baton taps a signal to begin
a breaking wave pins the chest, lifting higher
and out of their mouths, and strings and tubes and skins
ranging across octaves, energy spiralling
up from heels to crown through true centre
water swerving through its flow to flash, scouring
bedrock bare, curving a river bank, a tender
tacaneo drum roll flushes a heart unstitched
vibration coruscating, carving a cliff

If life after looping life

if time were
an arbitrary construct
existing only in our minds

understanding, a
shining globe coalescing
around an irritant,

our bodies, maps
scarred from falls,
chafing against restraints

the heart's hunger
to possess calling out,
jealous in this vacuum,

feet, calloused
from dead-end pilgrimage,
beached in this parched promised land.

If life after looping life
is spirit made flesh
sent out to repeat our purpose,

I would do this again and again